Nashua Public Library

Enjoy this book!
Please remember to return it on time
so that others may enjoy it too.

Manage your library account and
discover all we offer by visiting us
online at www.nashualibrary.org

Love your library? Tell a friend!

J

ENERGY EXCHANGE

TARA HAELLE

Rourke
Educational Media

rourkeeducationalmedia.com

Teaching Focus:

Have students locate the ending punctuation for sentences in the book. Count how many times a period, question mark, or exclamation point is used. Which one is used the most? What is the purpose for each ending punctuation mark? Practice reading these sentences with appropriate expression.

Before Reading:

Building Academic Vocabulary and Background Knowledge

Before reading a book, it is important to set the stage for your child or student by using pre-reading strategies. This will help them develop their vocabulary, increase their reading comprehension, and make connections across the curriculum.

1. *Look at the cover of the book. What will this book be about?*
2. *What do you already know about the topic?*
3. *Let's study the Table of Contents. What will you learn about in the book's chapters?*
4. *What would you like to learn about this topic? Do you think you might learn about it from this book? Why or why not?*
5. *Use a reading journal to write about your knowledge of this topic. Record what you already know about the topic and what you hope to learn about the topic.*
6. *Read the book.*
7. *In your reading journal, record what you learned about the topic and your response to the book.*
8. *After reading the book complete the activities below.*

Content Area Vocabulary

Read the list. What do these words mean?

chemical
coal
electricity
energy
fuel
radiation
solar
speed
thermal
transferred

After Reading:

Comprehension and Extension Activity

After reading the book, work on the following questions with your child or students to check their level of reading comprehension and content mastery.

1. *What kinds of energy are there? (Summarize)*
2. *Why do people need to use more renewable energy? (Infer)*
3. *What are some examples of things people use energy to do? (Asking Questions)*
4. *What would you miss the most if you didn't have electricity? (Text to Self Connection)*
5. *Why is the sun's energy important? (Asking Questions)*

Extension Activity

What are some ways you can conserve energy in your home and community? Design a poster that encourages people to save energy and gives them tips on how to do so. See if a local business will display your poster.

Table of Contents

Making Things Happen

How long can you run or sing or even stay awake before you get tired? No one can do these activities forever. Eventually, you run out of **energy**. Energy makes things happen. Energy is the ability to move and do work.

Energy is around us all the time. It's in sunlight, in wind, in our homes, and our bodies. People use energy to do all kinds of work, from driving cars to heating homes.

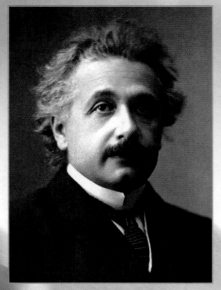

Explaining Energy

Scientists who study the physical world, including energy, are called physicists. A great physicist of the 20th century was Albert Einstein (1879–1955). He explained how energy works in the universe.

Energy exists in two basic forms: kinetic energy and potential energy. Kinetic energy is energy in motion. A ball rolling or a car whizzing by are examples of kinetic energy. Potential energy is stored energy.

Amazing Physicist
One of the greatest physicists was Marie Curie (1867–1934). She was the first woman to win a Nobel Prize in science, the world's top science award. And she won it twice!

Imagine taking a rubber band and stretching it as far as you can. If you let go, the rubber band shoots across the room. Stretching it stores up potential energy.

Potential energy gets changed, or converted, into kinetic energy when you release the band and it travels across the room. **Fuel**, such as gasoline for a car, also contains potential energy. That energy gets released by burning the fuel.

Potential Energy

Kinetic Energy

LET'S GET MOVING

The faster something moves, the more energy it has. How fast it travels is its **speed**. For example, a cheetah racing through the African savannah has more speed and more energy than a tortoise crawling through the desert.

The larger something is, the more energy it has too. So a train traveling the same speed as a cheetah has a lot more energy than the cheetah does.

It's Electric!
All animals' bodies create electrical energy, but some animals, like electric eels and rays, use **electricity** to hunt or defend themselves. Others hunt by sensing electrical energy from their prey.

Sometimes energy gets used up, such as the cheetah getting tired and stopping to rest or the train running out of fuel. But energy can also move somewhere else. A baseball thrown by a pitcher contains a lot of energy until SMACK! — the catcher catches it in his mitt. Where did all that energy go? It was **transferred**.

When two objects collide, some energy is transferred, or moves, from one object to another and some energy is released. When the ball hits the catcher's glove, the SMACK! sound is the release of energy. The rest of the ball's energy is transferred to the catcher. OUCH!

The Speed of Light
Light is the fastest energy in the universe. It travels 186,000 miles (300,000 kilometers) per second. Traveling the speed of light, you would circle Earth 7.5 times in one second!

When the baseball hits the catcher's glove, some of it is transferred to the catcher in the form of heat. That's why a catcher's glove gets hot after catching pitch after pitch.

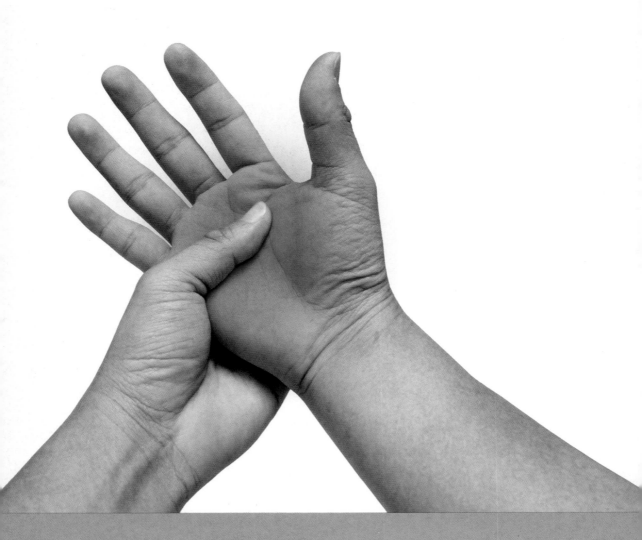

But what if a batter hits the ball? CRACK! Some energy is released as sound, and some energy is transferred from the ball to the bat. But the ball keeps some of its energy too. It also receives some energy from the swinging bat. Energy is exchanged between the ball and bat, and the ball soars into the outfield.

Pendulums of Kinetic & Potential Energy

Two objects can often transfer energy back and forth to one another. You can create a set of pendulums to show this.

You will need:
- string or yarn
- two rubber bouncy balls
- masking or duct tape
- table
- ruler
- smooth stick, such as a wooden dowel stick

Instructions:

1. Measure and cut two pieces of string that are exactly 15 inches (38.1 centimeters).

2. Tape one end of one string to one bouncy ball. Make sure it's taped securely. Tape the other string to the other ball. Compare the strings to see if they are still the same length. You may need to trim one to make them the same. You've made two pendulums.

3. Tape exactly one inch (2.54 centimeters) of one pendulum's string onto the top of the table. Tape exactly one inch (2.54 centimeters) of the other pendulum's string to the table six inches (15.24 centimeters) away from the first pendulum.

4. At four inches (10.16 centimeters) below the table, wrap both pendulums' strings once around the stick to secure the stick between them. The stick should be perfectly horizontal. You may need tape to secure the string.

5. Take one pendulum and pull it out to the side of the other so that it hits the other pendulum when you let go. Watch as each pendulum hits the other and transfers its energy to the other pendulum.

The moving pendulum has kinetic energy. When it hits the other pendulum, that energy is transferred. Each time one pendulum hits the other, a tiny bit of energy is released as sound. The pendulums can keep transferring energy back and forth until all the energy has escaped from the collisions.

How Energy Travels

Sound is just one way energy moves. Light, heat, and electricity are other forms of energy or ways to transfer energy.

Heat energy is called **thermal** energy. Thermal energy can travel in three ways: **radiation**, conduction, and convection. Radiation is energy traveling in waves. Energy traveling as light or sound also travels in waves.

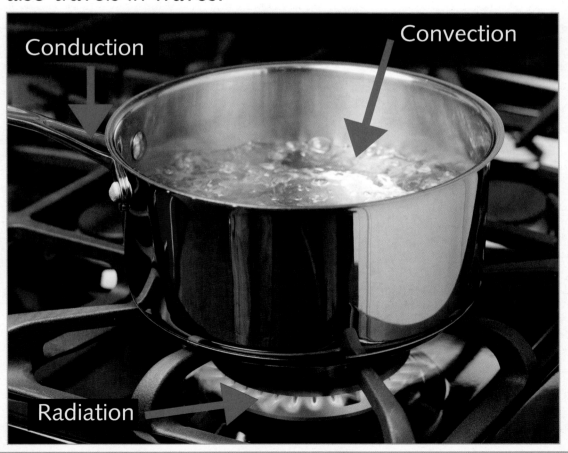

Conduction

Convection

Radiation

Conduction moves energy by having one object touch another. Wrapping a heated blanket around you when you're cold transfers thermal energy to your body and warms it up.

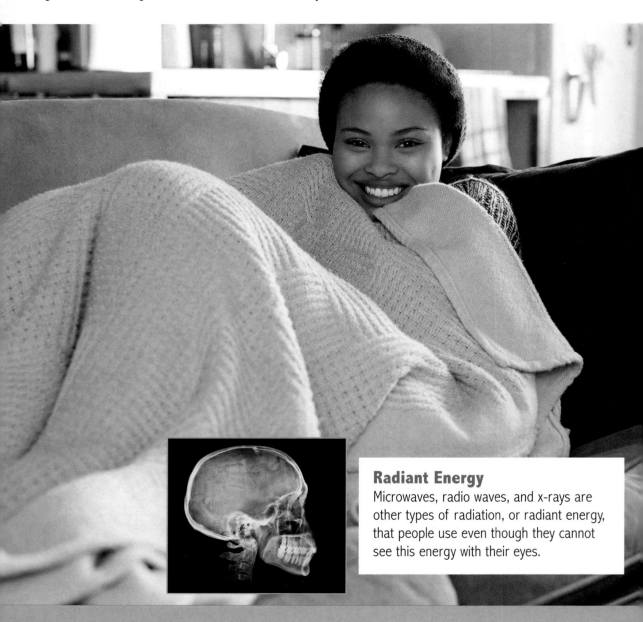

Radiant Energy
Microwaves, radio waves, and x-rays are other types of radiation, or radiant energy, that people use even though they cannot see this energy with their eyes.

Convection is the transfer of energy through air or through a liquid. Heat moves from a hotter area to a colder area. Steam coming off hot tea or hot chocolate is convection. Hot air balloons also work through convection. A balloon pilot heats the air inside the balloon. The hot air inside the balloon makes the balloon rise.

Which Materials Conduct Heat Best?

A conductor is a material that transfers energy. Some materials are better than others in transferring thermal energy. Let's find out which ones.

You will need:

hot tap water (with an adult's help)
wooden bowl
glass bowl
metal bowl
towel
wooden cutting board
plastic cutting board
metal pan
glass pan
freezer

Instructions:

1. Set each bowl on the counter and put your hand on the side to feel the temperature.

2. Fill each of the bowls with hot tap water. Wait 60 seconds.

3. Dump the water out of each bowl carefully and then turn the bowls upside down on a towel.

4. Carefully move your hand close to each bowl to feel the heat. If it's not too hot, place your hand on each bowl. What do you notice about the three bowls? Which one got the hottest? Why?

5. Place the metal pan, the glass pan, and the cutting boards in the freezer and leave them for an hour.

6. Take out the pans and cutting boards and put them on the counter. Place your hand on top of each one. What do you notice? Which one is absorbing the heat from your hand the fastest? Why?

No matter where or how energy travels, it never disappears. In fact, the amount of energy in our universe always stays exactly the same. Nothing can create energy, and nothing can destroy energy. It simply moves around.

Sound in Space
Sound can only travel through a substance, such as water or air. But outer space is a vacuum, an area with nothing in it. So sound cannot travel in space!

Electricity Makes Power

One of the most common ways people move energy around is electric energy, or electricity. The movement of electric energy is called a current. The energy carried in electrical currents can then be changed into other forms of energy to create sound, light, heat, or motion.

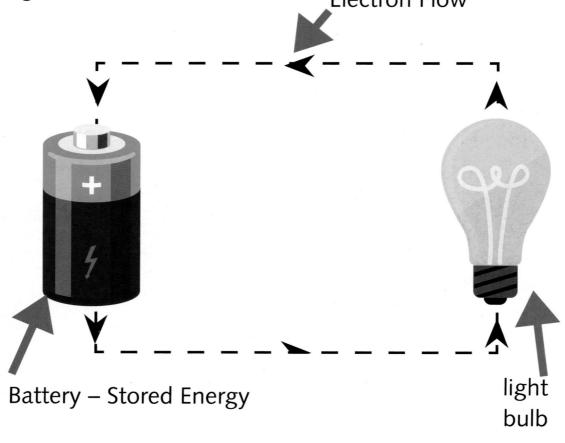

Electron Flow

Battery – Stored Energy

light bulb

Electricity is a flow of electrons around a circuit.

Insulator
Does not conduct electricity
- toothpick
- cardboard
- rubber
- Q-tip
- clothes pin

Conductor
Conducts electricity
- penny
- paper clip
- aluminum
- nickel
- nail
- key

Conductors

Electricity also moves through conduction. A material that transfers that energy is a conductor. Metal and water are good conductors. Wood and plastic are not.

For example, electricity can provide power to play music on a phone or computer. When you turn on a light switch, electricity is converted into light. An electric stove uses electricity to create heat to cook food. Electricity can create motion by providing power for a fan to cool a room.

But how do people create electricity? They have to get the energy from somewhere else and change it into electric power. People get energy from an energy source. One source is **chemical** energy.

Dry wood is a source of chemical energy. Burning the wood converts the chemical energy into thermal energy (heat) and light energy.

Benjamin Franklin
1706–1790

Thomas Edison
1847–1931

Bright Discoveries

Two Americans made important discoveries about electricity. Benjamin Franklin discovered lightning is electric energy, and Thomas Edison invented the first light bulb. Edison's electric company lit up New York City in 1882.

Chemicals are all the substances that make up the universe. When they interact with each other, they can give off energy, just as two things colliding give off energy. Batteries use chemical energy to create electrical currents. But many other sources of energy exist too.

All Kinds of Energy

People get most energy from fossil fuels. Oil, **coal**, and natural gas are all fossil fuels that formed from the remains of dead plants and animals millions of years ago.

Burning oil, coal, and gas releases energy. But once a lump of coal is burned, there is no way to replace it. One day, the Earth will run out of fossil fuels.

Non-Renewable Energy
Fossil Fuel Oil
Coal
Natural Gas

That's why people are now using more energy sources that never get completely used up. These sources can be replaced, or renewed. Three major sources of renewable energy include sunlight, wind, and water.

Renewable Energy

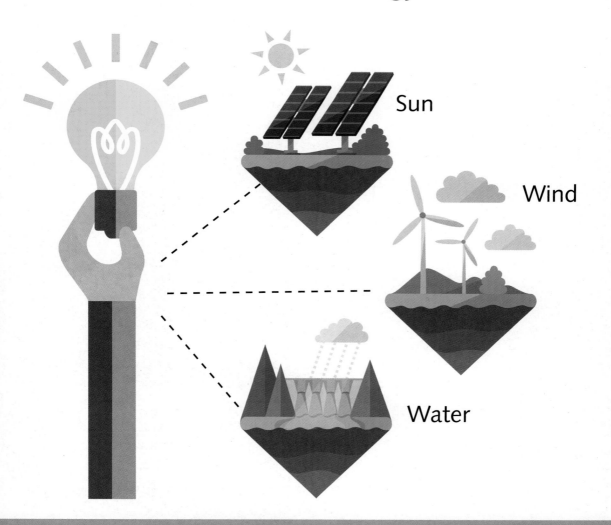

Sun

Wind

Water

Energy from the sun is called **solar** energy. Solar energy sustains all life on Earth. Plants convert solar energy into sugar so they can use it. People can turn solar energy into electricity.

Making Electricity

A power plant is a factory that converts energy into electricity. The largest solar power plant in the world is in the Mojave Desert in California.

Wind is another renewable energy source. People use windmills to capture the energy of the wind moving a windmill's blades around. The windmill converts that energy into a form people can use.

Water flowing in a river has kinetic energy. If a beaver builds a dam, water builds up behind the dam and becomes potential energy. Water flowing over the dam releases that energy.

People-Made Power

Hoover Dam sits on the Nevada-Arizona border just outside Las Vegas. When it was built in 1936, it was the tallest dam in the United States. Today, it's the second tallest after Oroville Dam in Northern California.

People also build dams to generate electricity from that energy. Using renewable energy sources means people will never run out of energy!

GLOSSARY

chemical (KEM-i-kuhl): a substance used in or made by chemistry, as in household chemicals

coal (kohl): a black mineral formed from the remains of ancient plants; coal is mined underground and burned as a fuel

electricity (i-lek-TRIS-i-tee): a form of energy caused by the motion of electrons and protons

energy (EN-ur-jee): the ability of something to do work; energy is a concept in physics and is measured in joules

fuel (FYOO-uhl): something that is used as a source of heat or energy, such as coal, wood, gasoline, or natural gas

radiation (ray-dee-AY-shuhn): the giving off of energy in the form of light or heat

solar (SOH-lur): of or having to do with the sun or powered by energy from the sun

speed (speed): the rate at which someone or something moves

thermal (THUR-muhl): of or having to do with heat or holding in heat

transferred (TRANS-furred): moved someone or something from one person or place to another

Index

Show What You Know

1. What are the two basic types of energy?
2. Why is there usually a sound when two things hit each other?
3. What is energy called if it travels in waves?
4. How does conduction move energy?
5. What does it mean if energy is renewable?

Websites to Visit

www.eia.gov/kids

www.energyquest.ca.gov/story/chapter01.html

climatekids.nasa.gov/menu/energy

About the Author

Tara Haelle spent much of her youth exploring creeks and forests outside and reading books inside. Her adventures became bigger when she became an adult and began traveling across the world on exciting adventures such as swimming with sharks, climbing Mt. Kilimanjaro, exploring the Amazon, and eating insects! She earned a master's degree in photojournalism from the University of Texas at Austin so she could keep learning about the world by talking to scientists and writing about their work. She currently lives in central Illinois with her husband, two sons, two Chihuahuas, and two cats. You can learn more about her at www.tarahaelle.net.

Meet The Author!
www.meetREMauthors.com

www.rourkeeducationalmedia.com

PHOTO CREDITS: Cover and title page: ©Digitalsignal; table of contents: ©chinaface; p.4, 16: ©Squaredpixels; p.5: ©RapidEye; p.6: ©Paul Velgos; p.7: ©gpointstudio, ©zbruch; p.8: ©Graeme Purdy; p.9: ©&#169 hfng, ©wrangel; p.10: ©joshblake; p.11: ©Cheryl Quigley; p.12: ©stlee000; p.13: ©Tomwang112; p.15: ©RyersonClark; p.16: ©daboost; p.17: ©ImagesbyTrista, ©studiocasper; p.19: ©Hayri Er; p.21: ©EHSTock; p.22: ©Muravin; p.24: ©Ralf Hettler; p.26: ©CrackerClips; p.27: ©Rawpixel Ltd; p.28: ©johnnya123; p.29: ©powerofforever

Edited by: Keli Sipperley
Cover design by: Rhea Magaro-Wallace
Interior design by: Kathy Walsh

Library of Congress PCN Data

Energy Exchange / Tara Haelle
(Science Alliance)
ISBN 978-1-68342-349-2 (hard cover)
ISBN 978-1-68342-445-1 (soft cover)
ISBN 978-1-68342-515-1 (e-Book)
Library of Congress Control Number: 2017931193

Rourke Educational Media
Printed in the United States of America,
North Mankato, Minnesota